Alex Pottes
March 2007

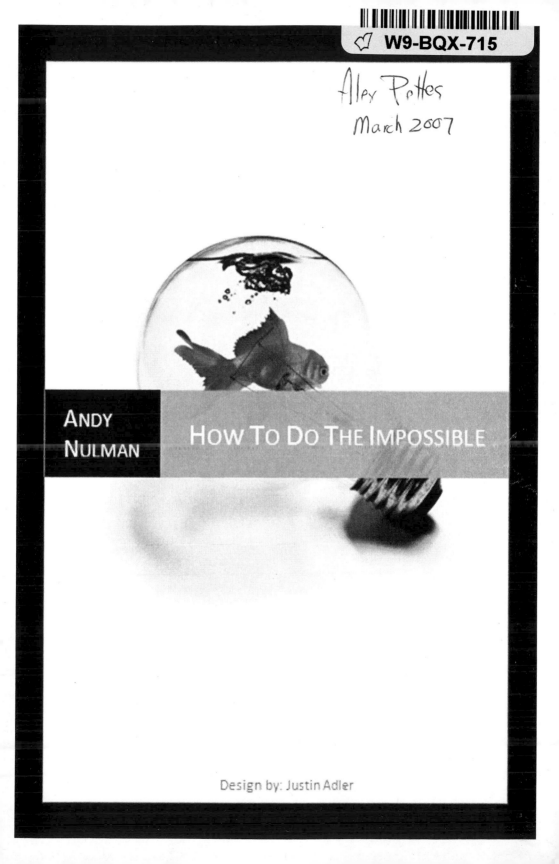

ANDY
NULMAN

HOW TO DO THE IMPOSSIBLE

Design by: Justin Adler

Published in 2007
Andy Nulman
First printing February 2007

Andy Nulman, 1959 –
How To Do The Impossible

ISBN 1896912-13-3
1. Goal (psychology). 2. Achievement motivation. I. Title
BF505.G6N8413 2007 158.1 C98-931439-1

Cover Design: Justin Adler
Cover and About the Author Photos: Heidi Hollinger

Printed in Canada

Acknowlegements

Writing a book is a true paradox; a bold individual act and a desperate reliance on others rolled into one. All this to say that without the support from the following people, I could've never even imagine myself barricaded in solitude to create what you now hold. So...

- Thank you to Justin Adler for bringing new life to the old manuscript. You are wise beyond your years, creative beyond my imagination and devious enough to edit your own acknowledgement and bring it up from the middle of the pack to the top.

- Thank you to two great friends and business partners that life has been kind enough to bring my way: Garner Bornstein and Gilbert Rozon, totally different in spirit and personality, but both brilliant, unique and generous.

- Thank you Heidi Hollinger. Your photo session was the first twist of fate in making this book a reality.

- Thank you to Salim Khoja of the Power Within for believing I'm good enough to share stages with Tony Robbins and Bill Clinton, and to bringing a voice to this book.

- For unconditional inspiration and love, I salute my father Norman and late mother Carol, my sister Nancy and brother Stuart, as well as my in-laws Faigie and Seymour, my brothers-in-law Steven, Howard and Henry and my sisters-in-law Gail and Joanne, and of course, Uncle Barry and Nicole, Ali, Hailey, Greggy, Justin and Laura.

- Finally, to the people who always made the office seem more like family than work, a big swing of the baseball bat to my long-time (and oft-suffering) assistant Diane Shatz, to Nancie Wight, Dennis McFern, Andrew Zeidel, Ion Valaskakis and Bessy Ziannis of Airborne and to Bruce Hills, Willie Mercer, Robin Altman, Marc Hamou, Suzanne Hinks and Jodi Lieberman of Just For Laughs.

For Aidan Foster
and Hayes Brody,
but especially for Ski.

Introduction "A"
What this Book Ain't

This is a business book.

It's also a self-help book.

It's a motivational tome, a social commentary and a bit of an autobiography rolled into one.

It's personal (_really_ personal), it's emotional, it's inspirational and it's practical.

Despite its triumphant, grandiose title it's a simple book.

All this aside, here's the best thing about this book:

It Ain't Fat.

It ain't fat not because I'm lazy, and despite my admiration of Al Gore, not because I'm some sort of conservationist worried about forests or trees (it's printed on recycled stock anyway, so there!).

It ain't fat...because I want you to _actually_ read it.

That doesn't sound like much of a challenge, but it is. Just look at your bookshelf.

Books bought with all the good intention in the world. How many of them remain half-read or, worse yet, never opened? How many lulled you to sleep with charts, tables, graphs and other tools of boredom? How many overwhelmed you with evidence, experiments and theories until you cried out in frustration:

"Yeah, but what does this mean for me?"

How many of them looked, felt, sounded like the same ol' song and dance?

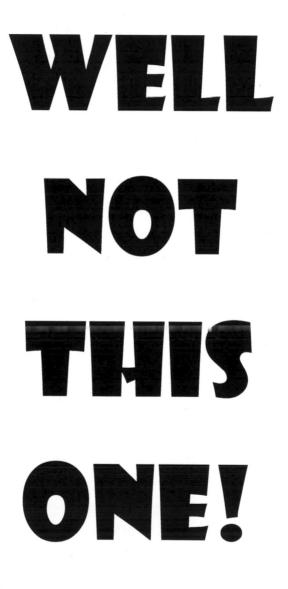

WELL NOT THIS ONE!

Because this one *ain't* fat.

There are just four chapters. And just four main points. Powerful points mind you, but just four of 'em

So raise your glasses and toast to simplicity! Strike up the band! Just four points! No pie charts! No bar graphs! No goofy workbooks or exercises! No lists to make or promises to break...uh, keep. This ain't about me impressing you about how smart I am; it's about you impressing yourself about extraordinary you can be! This book ain't fat because I want you to use what's in it. It ain't fat because before you know it, you'll be through it.

It was written to be fully consumed in one sitting; two at the very most. After which you can go out and start doing the impossible.

Because who wants to read about something this exciting when you can actually do it for yourself?

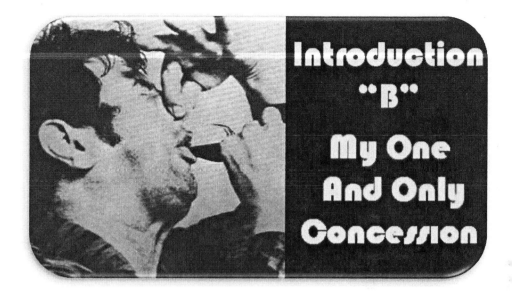

Introduction "B"
My One And Only Concession

Okay, so you prefer a more conventional introduction then the "Ain't Fat" explanation.

Well, you've got your wish. But I'm warning you, this is the *last* concession I'm making in this book.

You want conventional? Buy someone else's book. Things are going to be done differently within these pages. This one's about doing the *impossible*, not doing the *ordinary*.

And ironically, the distance between the two is really not that great. This I learned young. The notion of impossibility has intrigued me since 4th Grade, all starting with the then mind-bending concept of long-division. Every time I voiced frustration about my astounding ineptitude with long division, whining "This is impossible!" with every example given to me, my math teacher Mrs. Barmash would snap a bony finger in my face and chide me with stern refrains of:

"Nothing is impossible, young man!"

To disprove Mrs. Barmash's academic dogma, my friends and I would get together and concoct some of the most preposterous and outrageous physical challenges in an attempt to find the truly not-doable and to ridicule our teacher in the process. (Hey, to rebel, some kids smoked in alleys; we concocted the impossible.)

And concoct we did. In retrospect, they're silly, but to a fourth-grade mind, these were postulations of future shock:

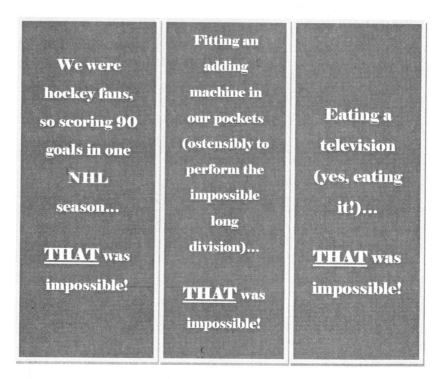

We were hockey fans, so scoring 90 goals in one NHL season...

THAT was impossible!

Fitting an adding machine in our pockets (ostensibly to perform the impossible long division)...

THAT was impossible!

Eating a television (yes, eating it!)...

THAT was impossible!

With further hindsight, they're not all merely silly...they've also all been accomplished. Wayne Gretzky scored 92 goals in the 1982-83 NHL season. Adding machines are now calculators, and fit on the ends of pens. Yes, even chowing down a complete television – with a bicycle as an appetizer – has been done. It was a stunt performed by Mr. Mange-Tout (the stage name meaning "Mr. Eat-All" of Michel Lotito, of Grenoble, France) over a weekend at the Carrefour Laval shopping center, just outside Montreal, in 1979.

What's more, I can now long-divide with the best of them. By hand, yet!

Big deal you say? It is a big deal. In fact, it's the underlying theme of this book:

Impossible is a present-day perspective

Nothing seems impossible when you look back upon it, only when you look ahead to it. You see, to do the impossible, all you have to do is put your mind...

Whoa

Whoa

Whoa!

That's a little too much information for an introduction, especially an "alternative" introduction I'm writing against my will. Like long-division, doing the impossible is quite elementary, once you learn all the tricks. I could go on, but I'd be taking a serious chunk out of my very important Chapter 2. Be patient, dear reader. You'll get there before you know it.

But before I let you go, let me regale you with some remarkably astute words from the wise:

Smart People, Smart Talk
(Yeah, Right...)

"Everything that can be invented has been invented."
- Charles H. Duell
Commissioner of U.S. Office of Patents
1899

"Well-informed people know it is impossible to transmit the voice over wires and that were it possible to do so, the thing would be of no practical value."
- Editorial in the Boston Post
1865

"There is not the slightest indication that (nuclear) energy will ever be obtainable."
- Dr. Albert Einstein
1932

"The Japanese auto industry isn't likely to carve out a big slice of the U.S. market for itself."
- Business Week
August 2, 1968

"Heavier-than-air flying machines are impossible."
- Lord Kelvin
British Physicist and Mathematician
1895

"Nobody can overthrow me. I have the support of 700,000 troops, all the workers, and most of the people. I have the power."
- The Shah of Iran
March 6, 1978

"We don't think they'll do anything in this market."
- Alan Livingston, President of Capitol Records
Commenting on The Beatles
1964

"The Internet? We are not interested in it."
- Bill Gates
1993

"There's no way you I could ever _____."
- You
Today

Now, it's your moment of truth: turn the page and start reading so that you will make the final quote as ridiculous as the eight that preceded it.

Chapter 1.
You Are Not Normal!

You are not normal.

OUCH!

As an insult, the four little words **"You are not normal"** rang powerful and proved highly effective throughout my formative years. Fitting in was "in," thus the epitome of achievement was to be considered "normal." To make matters worse, its antonym, "abnormal," conjured up visions of circus freaks, sideshow geeks and people kept out of sight in Tupperware containers.

Things actually got worse as I got older and, presumably, better educated. After years of reading about student revolution of the '60s, I was extremely disappointed to discover that modern-day university life was about as liberating as Henry Ford's assembly lines. Incidentally, a great tell-tale quote about schooling can be found in Roger von Oech's eternally-outstanding book *A Whack on the Side of the Head* (one which I read instead of my prescribed textbooks back in Vanier College):

> *We enter school as a "?"*
> *and we leave as a "."*

(I think I left as a "...")

Anyway, I went through university accompanied by pals like Scholastic Aptitude Tests and Bell Curves; devices that reward those who fell within predetermined limits of normality. And heaven help those unfortunate souls who landed outside he established parameters! They became grown-up versions of those unruly kids who dared to colour outside the lines, or couldn't stay within them no matter how hard they tried. Subsequently, they were pitied, shunned and ostracized. They were laughed at, picked on and ridiculed.

And they've become Steve Jobs, Sergey Brin and Larry Page, Sir Richard Branson, Chad Hurley and Steve Chen and other people we now admire...or envy.

And the "normal" people? They buy iPods, use Google, fly Virgin Atlantic, use Virgin Mobile and post videos on YouTube.

I think by now you must be getting the point:

Normal people do not do the impossible; normal people do normal things.

Therefore, by applying a simple associative mathematics theory (one I learned after conquering long division, of course):

To do
the impossible,
you can't be
normal.

So if you can accept the notion that you are not normal, if you can accept the title of this chapter as a compliment rather than an insult, then you're ready to do the impossible.

Now I know it's not going to be easy. What I'm asking you to do is, in one fell swoop, reject years of preconditionning from parents, teachers, friends, family, clergy, doctors and lovers...then take a leap of faith and accept a new gospel from yours truly. All within a few pages.

That's not normal!

Well, ain't that my point exactly!

Okay, let me make it easier for you. Let's look in the dictionary, as "normal" a reference as one could imagine. Here's how the Merriam Webster's Collegiate Dictionary, in its 2003 edition, defined the dreaded n-word:

> Nor•mal: conforming to a type, standard or regular pattern; of relating to, or characterized by average intelligence or development; free from mental disorder.

Now is that not a definition from hell? Conforming. Standard. Regular. Augggghhhhh! It's the nightmare vision from the Pete Seeger song Little Boxes:

> *And they all fit into boxes.*
> *Little boxes.*
> *Just the same.*

(As an aside, another dictionary, the New Shorter Oxford English Dictionary, published in 1993, listed "heterosexual" as one of its defining terms of "normal." Oy...)

Ok, let's take a look at the flip-side, it too from Merriam Webster's:

> **Ab•nor•mal**: different from the norm or average, unusual, not typical; contrary to rule, deviating from a recognized standard; exceptional.

Unusual. Not typical. Exceptional. Now doesn't that make you feel better?

Or let me put it another way...what would you consider a better compliment from a member of the opposite sex? (Or even from a member of the same sex, New Shorter Oxford Dictionary be damned!) Being described as average or standard, or being described as exceptional, different, unique?

So you see, "You are not normal" is no insult; it's actually quite the tribute to your exceptional character traits, to your potential to do the impossible.

Therefore, by association, abnormal is good. Let me restate it:

Abnormal is Good!

Write it down somewhere. Aw, forget it, let me do it for you. Tear out the next page and put it where it will stare you in the face every day.

Good! is Abnormal

Immortal is Good!

You want to do the impossible? Then stop thinking normal and start embracing abnormality. In the words of Tom Peters, one of our generation's top business thinkers:

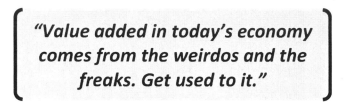

"Value added in today's economy comes from the weirdos and the freaks. Get used to it."

So start adding value to the economy. Start adding value to your day-to-day existence. And stop worrying about what others will say. They'll come along nipping at your heels, asking for jobs and favors...once you surpass them.

Yes, abnormal is good. But I can't feel that you still aren't 100% convinced. Well, I can't waste precious paper and ink with another page of giant writing, so consider the following:

<u>Here's what normal people do</u>

• accept what they're given

• believe what they're told

• never challenge the odds

• resign themselves to fate

• act rationally

If everyone were normal, there would be no artists, no scientists, no Olympic champions, no politicians (hmmmm, on second thought...)

If everyone were normal, there would be no laptop computers, no medical breakthroughs, nothing to make you laugh or cry.

If everyone were normal, there would be no future.

(And if everyone were normal, there would be no one buying this book. So thank God for abnormality!)

Wanna talk abnormal? Do you think the Steves—Wozniak and Jobs—were normal when (as teenagers!) they cobbled together a bunch of electronic junk in a California garage and decided that they would take on IBM? And take them on they did, as their Apple Computer begot the personal computer revolution.

Apple has never shied away from its "abnormal" roots. In fact, the company's 1997/98 ad campaign, my fave, bore the slogan "Think Different" and paid homage to people like Einstein, Picasso and Gandhi, amongst others; "the crazy ones" as Apple put it. By the way, guess which computer I use?

So you think Jim Abbott was normal when he set his sights on playing major league baseball? Sure, thousands of kids have the same dream, but very few, if any of them, have only one arm. Yup, just one arm to do everything with – throw, catch, hit, field, block his ears form disbelievers and their slurs. Can you imagine the cruel comments and snide remarks when Abbott would share his dream?

"Yeah, a one-armed pitcher. What's next? A one-legged place-kicker?" Yet Abbott made it. And he made it not as some freak or publicity stunt or "Hire the handicapped" poster boy. He made it as a star with the New York Yankees and the California Angels. When he played in the National

League with the Milwaukee Brewers, he actually got up to bat!

Do you think Guy Laliberté was normal when the penniless fire-eater and street performer talked of reinventing the traditional circus, the animal-and-clown shows that had roots for hundreds of years? In 1985, his Cirque du Soleil couldn't draw more than 75 customers into its 1,500-seat tent. Today, Laliberté's moving musical/visual masterpiece has four permanent shows in Las Vegas (where it did the impossible by changing the city's entertainment feel from tacky to artsy), ten shows a-touring (with three more on the way) and most importantly, is changing the standard against which all live performance is measured. And it's paid off for him pretty well, too; Guy's a billionaire a few times over.

Abnormal? Sir Richard Branson is practically the poster child for the abnormal movement. The father of all things

Virgin, he started up a record label, an airline, a mobile phone company, a railroad, bridal shops and dozens of other businesses (I can go on for pages) without any previous experience in the fields (hence the "Virgin" moniker). His newest endeavors—alternative fuel and space travel; the former ostensibly to help power the latter. And his motto, his call to action when beseeched by the naysayers—"Screw it. Let's do it!"

And how about Howard Schultz? Think he was normal when he wanted to change America's coffee culture from "instant" to "social"? He wanted to give Americans a personal coffee experience, the type he experienced at espresso bars in Italy. Would never work, he was told; Americans like their coffee cheap, weak and fast. So he founded a company now known as Starbucks. Never mind coffee; Starbucks is now one of largest food service companies in world, has spawned dozens of imitators, and is using it's massive reach and connection to sell music, film, and social causes.

And it's where I'm sitting to edit the manuscript you are now reading.

The most unforgettable people are those who never let reality get in their way. Garage geeks who wanna conquer one of the world's largest companies. One-armed kids who wanna star in the big leagues. Flat-broke fire-eaters who wanna entertain the world. Merchants who won't settle for the boring status quo. I could go on and on with examples. But what would you rather do:

Read examples...or set examples?

You may be asking yourself "Yeah, but what about the odds?" Screw the odds! They're for normal people to consider. Do you know the odds are on making it big in Hollywood? Miniscule, that's what! Here's a bone chilling fact: according to the Screen Actors Guild, approximately 60% of its 86,000 members make less than $15,000 a year from acting.

Despite this, laughing in the face of the impossible odds, thousands of young hopefuls from all over the world descend upon Hollywood every month. And inevitably, every month you hear of some new star, coming out of Nowheresville, achieving seemingly instant fame and fortune. (Of course they're going to make it; their abnormality prevents them form realizing that they can't.) Take that, odds!

Perhaps actress Laura Linney put it best when she told Fortune Magazine: "There's good reason parents tell their children not to go into acting. The ratio of success to failure is daunting. But the need to perform outweighs rational thinking."

If you can accept that abnormality is actually a good thing, you've jumped over the first hurdle. But accepting abnormal and being abnormal are not the same thing. To do the impossible, you're going to have to THINK abnormal...which is actually easier done than said. (Go ahead, say it to yourself. Sounds crazy, right? Just don't say it too loud.)

In its simplest form, thinking abnormal can be tested by what I like to call "The Classic Glass of Water Conundrum."

Take a look at it, and ask yourself the following question:

Is the glass half-empty, or half-full?

Normal Thinkers see it as either one of these two conventional options and move on. They've got things to do, people to bore.

"Advanced" Normal Thinkers "get the trick." They see it as half-empty, AND as half-full, at the same time! Wow! Isn't that nifty? They can see one thing, two different ways!!! Wow! Call a press conference! Alert the military!

Sorry guys, you ain't got what it takes to do the impossible. Enjoy the rest of your lives.

To do the impossible, you have to think abnormally. Abnormal Thinkers are people who look at the same thing as everyone else, but see something different. Abnormal thinkers are a different species. They look at the glass and wonder:

•Who poured the water?
•Did they pour it half-full, or did they fill it to the brim and let it evaporate?
•Did someone drink it down to half?
•Who designed the glass? Karim Rashad? Phillipe Starck? Wal-Mart?
•Is it glass, or is it plastic, or Baccarat crystal?
• Is there really water in there? Or is it vodka? Or turpentine? Or—GASP!—liquid explosives?

Add about 5,000 more questions here...

See what I mean? Normal thinking stops once you answer the question. Abnormal thinkers see an answer as a pathway to other questions.

Here's another example: I'm slowly losing the hearing in my left ear. As a rock 'n' roll journalist from the age of 16 to 23, I was out at concerts almost every night. The end result of such aural abuse is a little medical condition called Otosclerosis, which has limited my hearing...and which is why I subtly turn to my right when in conversation.

Now I can accept my condition or I can change it. I've been given two possible solutions to the problem—an operation or a hearing-aid. And I've eschewed both; the former for the risk (a 50:50 chance that it will work wonders or completely cut off hearing to the ear), the latter because of the stigma attached to wearing one.

But then I think, I think abnormally...and I realize that hearing is one of the five senses. Many people suffer from diminishing functioning of another one of the five senses: sight. They, too, can change their predicament by having an operation, or wearing a "seeing-aid," namely eye-glasses.

My whole point here is that there's less of a stigma attached to wearing glasses as opposed to wearing a hearing aid. Glasses can be cool; not so hearing aids. Why? Maybe I can convince Giorgio Armani to create a line of designer hearing aid, with his winged logo sticking out of my ear-drum. Maybe I could start a new trend, a new industry...[*]

Or maybe not. But a least I'm thinking abnormally. And I'm challenging conventional wisdom. The mind is at work.

I think the United Negro College Fund said it best with their fund-raising slogan – "A mind is a terrible thing to waste." And waste ours we do with normal thinking.

There's a statistic I always come across, something to the effect that we can only use 10% of our thinking capacity. What's worse, we don't even use that 10% properly!

The mind is a powerful tool; but like other tools, it goes to waste if simply left to hang on a pegboard in a basement workshop. To do the impossible, you've got to stretch the limitations of your mind, and harness the power it has over your body, over others, over your future.

---

[*] Incidentally, it's exactly what is going on as this is being written. But instead of Armani, one of my co-conspirators in this endeavor is hearing health maverick Nick Laperle. His company Sonomax sent shockwaves through a staid and ultra-conservative industry when he announced a deal with Wal-Mart to do for hearing-aids within their stores what LensCrafters has done in malls throughout the continent: custom fit 'em and deliver them within one hour at a value price.

The other co-conspirators are artist Frank Cipra and jeweler David Maidor. They've been playing around with Sonomax prototypes for a few months. Frank paints the wild designs on masks for the majority of NHL goaltenders, and has shrunk his canvas somewhat to detail my potential hearing aid with skulls, bombs exploding and other less-than-subtle imagery. David, who custom-makes baubles for the rich and famous, is working to fit Nick's technology into a white gold shell, which he will (hopefully) cover in pave diamonds. In a nutshell—I need one, and I'll wear one…but only as art or jewelry.

I've started you off with the glass of water example. Now it's up to you to take this further. Yeah, you. That person staring back at you in the mirror. Did you think that this book was gonna do the impossible for you? It's your turn to exercise the abnormality of your thinking with other objects, with other situations. Ask "What If?" Ask "How Come?" Ask "why Not?" Ask "Who put the bomp in the bomp-shoo-bop?"

You can do it while driving (*"What if the road was made of rubber and tires of cement?"*). You can do it while sitting in dreary meetings *("How would I redesign this boardroom table to make meetings more exciting?"*). You can do it on Friday night at the in-laws' for dinner *("What would I rather be eating right now? Where would I rather be eating right now?"*).

Tear down all preconceived notions. Challenge all rules and regulations. Break the law of gravity. Turn reality inside out. No one will stop you! Abnormal Thinking has been described as mental masturbation—it's free, it's fun and it feels good. Believe me, the way it will enliven the boring parts of your life is alone worth the price of this book ten times over.

So screw the odds!
And screw normality!
And screw conformity!

We're abnormal!

AND WE'RE GONNA DO THE IMPOSSIBLE!

An
Afterword

Okay let's face the cold, hard facts.

You probably *won't* start another global, unique video community like Chad Hurley and Steve Chen did with YouTube. You probably *won't* change the live performance experience like Guy Laliberté did with Cirque du soleil. And, as for pitching in the majors like Jim Abbott, well, even with two good arms, uh, I don't think so.

But that doesn't mean you can't do the impossible. Au contraire; only you can establish exactly what "the impossible" is. What's impossible to some is routine to others. I bet you can do many things that, let's say, Bill Gates considers unachievable.

You see, defining "the impossible" is like defining "love" or faith" or "fun." "Impossible" is as subjective as a term can possibly be. You, your values, your wishes, your strengths and weaknesses all play a role in determining what "impossible" will be. It's an individual, personal challenge; not a shared, collective thing. It's what **YOU** want to do.

To some, "the impossible" will be as mundane as losing weight. To others, "the impossible" will be as ostentatious as running for public office. Whatever your "impossible" will be – from changing your pant size to changing the world – this book's simple, four step process will work for you.

What it won't work for are pipe dreams and fairytale wishes. "Oh, I wish I had a mansion in Monaco," is not doing the impossible; it's a fantasy. The mansion may be the reward for doing the impossible, but do it first, okay? Then claim your reward, thank you.

While taking a break from writing this book, I happened upon a national news report that was both inspiring and well-timed. It was about a school catering to a bunch of over-30 Canadians who had never before played hockey and wanted to take up the game.

These over-30s were a diverse bunch, ranging form immigrants who longed to participate in Canada's national sport, to well-off businessmen who never played because of family economic problems when they were kids.

Don't you think that the term "the impossible" flashed through their minds (not to mention their butts) the first time they stepped on the ice? Damn right it did. Don't you think that they're being thought of as crazy by various friends, family, and co-workers? Damn right they are. But don't you think they're going to get through the course, and keep playing the game? Damn right they will. Which goes to prove that in hockey, you don't have to be Wayne Gretzky or Sidney Crosby to do the impossible.

<u>Never forget</u>:

Doing the impossible is doing what YOU want to do.

And as for what I mentioned earlier, you know, an new Internet video idea, an earth-shattering live show concept, or throwing strikes in the Major Leagues...hey, if that's what the impossible really means to you, then take my second paragraph, tell me to shove it where the sun don't shine, and enjoy your challenge!

Who am I to tell to tell YOU what's impossible?

First the Bad News:

Not everyone can do the impossible.

Sorry.

It takes a special type of person to pull it off.

And now The Good News (well, you really didn't think I was going to leave you hanging on The Bad News, did you?):

This "special type of person" can be built. Assembled from the ground up.

And **YOU** can be one of 'em.

At this time, I would love to shout out in bold, flashing, 3D letters:

But I can't. **Because it's not.** Fact is, doing the Impossible is doable, but far from easy.

Yes, you can become an "Impossibilist", but it's gonna take work. And even prior to getting started on your quest of doing the Impossible, whatever yours may be, you have to bust butt to ensure that you possess the 10 traits unique to those who will actually be able to do it.

To that end, here's a concise and rather blunt list of Impossibilist Characteristics. Tick off the ones you are already lucky enough to have. Then get to work on developing the ones you need.

So, your journey to the Impossible is about to begin.

But first, a list of things to pack...

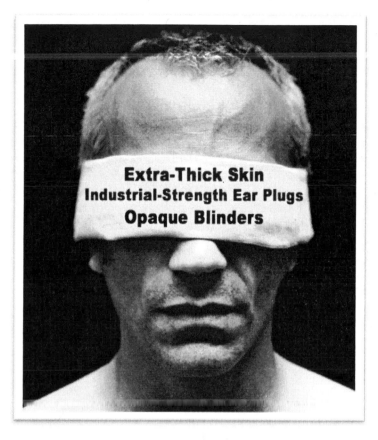

☐ **1) Extra-Thick Skin**
☐ **2) Industrial-Strength Ear Plugs**
☐ **3) Opaque Blinders**

The first three belong to the same family, hence their grouping together under an umbrella I like to call the **"Shield of Dreams."** Doing the Impossible involves proving others wrong. And since nobody really likes to be proven wrong, expect people to attack you with insults, jeers and the occasional pointed stick while going about your Impossibilist duties. As Michael Lewis (author off brainy business best-sellers like *Moneyball* and *The New New Thing*) puts it:

> *"Doing things differently is inherently threatening to people, because if it works, it's damning of the way they've been doing things (in the past)."*

Thus, points 1 and 2 should serve to protect you from the missiles fired and obstructions placed by your detractors. As for #3, no matter how intense your focus, life sometimes drops distractions in your path. If they are emergencies that need to be attended to, by all means attend to them. But if they are silly little diversions that will set you off course, be strong enough to ignore them and maintain focus.

☐ 4) A Love of Risk, Enjoyment of Gambling

Nope, this has nothing to do with trips to Vegas or buying lottery tickets. To do the Impossible, you're going to have to obliterate the odds and tap dance where others fear to tread. What's more, you must face this extreme uncertainty with a constant smile on your face. You win, you laugh; you lose, you chalk it up to experience and risk again. A little jittery and looking for a sure bet? That's not impossible, that's inconceivable.

☐ 5) Never Get Too Up, Never Get Too Down

Nothing lasts forever; not success, not failure. Life is a wild rollercoaster. Those who win ride it on an even keel throughout all its ups and downs. So smooth out your extremes—don't be an obnoxious braggart when you're flying and don't be despondent and suicidal when you're dying. Neither bathes you in an attractive light. Remember that the pendulum always swings the other way from whence it has come...and ultimately comes to rest in the middle. Control yourself.

☐ 6) A Certain Sense of Flamboyance

There's a big difference between the aforementioned obnoxious braggart and someone with flair. Choose the latter. Be out there...a little bit, at least. All Impossibilists are eventually looked up to, so choose to reflect the admiration with radiance. Let others bask in your style, in your glow, in your magnetism.

UNWAVERING BELIEF IN YOURSELF

☐ 7) Unwavering Belief in Yourself

Turbo-charge your self-confidence and upgrade your self-esteem. Doing the Impossible is rarely a solo act. Ultimately, you're going to have to get others to believe in you. And that's quite the formidable task if you don't believe in yourself first. You may be wearing the corporate outfit on the outside, but it had better be covering the Superman or Supergirl costume underneath.

☐ 8) Active Dreaming

Dreaming is the raw material, the catalyst to doing the Impossible. But it must be tempered. Robert Kennedy once famously pronounced:

> *"Some men see things as they*
> *are and say 'Why?'*
> *I dream things that never were*
> *and say 'Why not?'"*

To paraphrase RFK and bring his quote into an Impossibilist context, "Passive Dreamers (a.k.a. Daydreamers) dream and think 'What if?' Active Dreamers dream and think 'How?'" Get the difference?

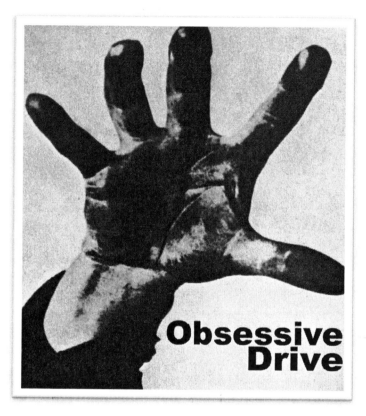

Obsessive Drive

☐ 9) Obsessive Drive

Doing the Impossible doesn't come to you; you have to go out and **GRAB IT** by the short-and-curlies, wrestle it to the ground, and hold it there while it resists. You've got to **LIVE** your Impossible to **DO** your Impossible. This may mean giving up some of the things, the activities, the people you enjoy. Such is life at the top. You don't do the Impossible part time, or by accident. You do it by diving in and being absorbed in it.

☐ 10) Unlimited Energy

Let's hear it for Red Bull and Starbucks, Official Fuels of the Impossibilist Movement! It's 4:12 a.m. and I'm still touching this up. I have a meeting in less than five hours. Get the picture? Watching the clock is for Nine-to-Fivers. Watching the calendar is for those with two weeks of vacation per year. Impossibilists have just one measure of time—the span between now…and achievement.

Loaded up with these 10 traits, there's one last thing you need to do: Check your watch. It's now-o-clock. Your Impossible is out there waiting for you.

Go get it!

Who the Hell Am I To Write This?

I ask you to take daunting leaps of faith. I implore you to reject things you've previously learned. To do the formidable, I urge you to accept my simple system.

Who the hell am I to expect all this?

Am I an academic? No, but I've taught many courses at the college and university level.

Am I a philosopher? No, but I'm not afraid to speak my mind. Even when I'm not asked.

Am I a guru? No, but hey, I did grow up in the '60s...man.

As CEO of the Just For Laughs International Comedy Festival, I helped develop the Montreal event into the largest, most important of its kind anywhere in the world.

With no previous experience, I produced (and many times wrote) its TV shows all over the globe. (And as an Anglophone, I ran one of Quebec's premiere French-language cultural events. Talk about doing the impossible!)

As President and CMO of Airborne Entertainment, I worked alongside partner and co-founder Garner Bornstein to start a business from scratch in a field that didn't exist (mobile media and entertainment) in North America.

A little more than five years after opening its doors, we sold 85% of Airborne—a company NOBODY believed in other than Garner and I—to a Japanese company called Cybird for over $110 million.

I could go on listing business accomplishments, but no matter how many I list, my business conquests alone don't qualify me to write this book.

So let's look at my sporting life. Yup, done my impossibles there, too.

At the age of 29, after being off skates since I was 12, I decided to take up hockey again...but this time as a goalie, a position I had never played. I strapped on the pads, got hit in the head a few times and was entranced by the thrill of making a save. Three years later, I took off a week from work and went to goalie camp, where I was the oldest "camper" by 14 years. While my bunkmates were talking about sneaking in beers, I was talking about my wife and kids. Today, I'm no Dominik Hasek (I'm not even Manon Rheaume!), but I still play competitively twice a week.

At the age of 35, with 35 years of hating winter under my belt, I decided to take up skiing. Today, I run to Vail, Colorado every winter to snowboard...an activity I undertook at the age of 36.

People laughed when I told them what I was going to do. They told me it couldn't be done...which only inspired me to do it more.

I could go on listing, sporting accomplishments, but that still doesn't qualify me to write this book.

Here's what does:

I've done the impossible many times. I've seen many others do it many times as well. Each time, I noticed an emerging pattern.

So I decided to do the impossible once again.

I would distill this pattern into four easy steps...and write an accessible book about it.

And can you believe it?

People rejected the idea. "They" (the all-powerful, ominous, ever-present "They") said it would never get published.

And if by some fluke it did, "They" said nobody would ever buy it.

Uh...can we move on now?

Don't Live FOR Tomorrow
Live IN Tomorrow!

Congratulations!

By venturing forth into Chapter 2, you have happily accepted the concept that you are not normal.

Now, you've got to prove it.

Hopefully, you've learned a new way to think. Now it's time to learn the secret of how to apply it. Like so much else that is valuable to our lives, this secret – the secret to doing the impossible – is simple, yet so complex.

Here it is:

To do the impossible, you've got to think it already done!

In other words, to do the impossible, you must not live **for** tomorrow, but **in** tomorrow. A subtle difference, yet an enormous one. The difference may be one single word on paper, but believe me, it's a quantum leap in your mind. And it's a quantum leap that gets easier and more controllable, with each successive attempt. (Remember: Normal Thinkers can't take quantum leaps in their heads. They have trouble just playing hop-scotch up there!)

In essence, what you will be doing is changing tense of your thinking. You'll be thinking back with confidence instead of thinking ahead with anxiety and uncertainty.

You see, the fundamental doubt people have in trying to do the impossible is the incessant worry about whether or not they can actually do it. But by living it tomorrow, the worry's gone. It's eliminated. Rendered obsolete. Finito.

The impossible has already been done...at least in your mind, it has. The outcome has been decided, and decided in your favor.

Just imagine the ultimate fate of James Cameron if his head was anywhere but the future while filming Titanic, which went on to become the top-grossing film of all time. Here was a guy writing a movie horribly late and over-budget, not one but two studios screeching at him, and the media poised with long knives ready to pounce on what they believed was about to become the biggest film flop of all time. Back then, there was only one rider on the Titanic bandwagon: Cameron himself.

To draw an analogy and help you understand, think back to those pencil mazes we used to unravel as kids.

Most of us (the Normal Thinkers!) would start where it said "Start" and wind our way through paths that led mostly to dead ends. A few re-starts (or jumped lines) and we wove our way towards the reward of the bold-lettered "Finish."

But some of us (you know who by now!) were thunderstruck with the idea of starting at the finish and winding our way back to finish at the start. And although we were solving the exact same problem, we were given the psychological edge of a different perspective – the perspective of guaranteed success. Hey, weren't we already at the finish line? No matter how complex and tangled the maze was, it always seemed easier to solve backwards from victory.

As I said a few pages ago in Introduction B – nothing seems impossible when you look back upon it. Not even long division. Again, let me repeat that **IMPOSSIBLE IS A PRESENT-DAY PERSPECTIVE.**

By changing that perspective, you automatically remove a great deal, if not all, of the stress that will impede your chances of doing the impossible. You obliterate your obstructions. You vault over your hurdles.

Because now, you're not longer worried IF you are going to do the impossible; now you're merely curious HOW you are going to do the impossible:

You're exchanging an if for a how.

You're exchanging worry for curiosity.

You're exchanging an uncertainty for a given.

People will look at you in amazement. They'll wonder why you're not totally stressed out. They'll remark how calm you seem, how you appear to be in complete and total control. And the more they toss out these compliments, the more motivated you'll become to accomplish your impossible.

So now, thanks to your abnormal thinking:

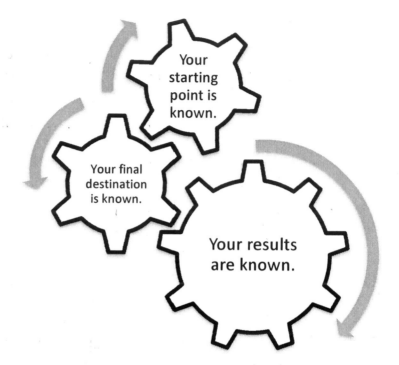

The only thing missing is the path. In which direction will your quantum leap take you? How high will you fly? Where's the turbulence along the way? Will there be unscheduled or emergency landings?

That's the next step in this chapter. But first, a little break. A pit-stop to get your head around the fact that it's going to be making like a Jules Verne contraption and travel through time. Here's a look at a couple of real-life examples of the "think it already done/live in tomorrow" hypothesis in action. (Did you really think I'd put forth such outlandish theories without showing you that it actually gets the job done?)

I bring you the real-life drama of Apollo 13. Life doesn't get more real then when it's at stake. Those of you who have seen the excellent film will remember this gut-wrenching scene vividly. To save the astronauts Jim Lovell, Jack Swigert and Fred Haise from a slow, cruel death by asphyxiation, scientists back on the ground at Houston had to create a working air-filter from a collection of odds and ends that the crew had in their possession miles above the earth, in outer space.

This was a literal example of fitting a square peg in a round hole. It was a bunch of stuff — plastic bags, duct tape, cardboard, hoses — poured onto a desk at Mission Control. It was an impossible confrontation; a pile of junk against poisonous carbon dioxide.

Interior of the Apollo 13 ship, showing the improvised part.

But there was no "Can we do it?" There was no "If we only had more time..." There was no "Wow, wouldn't this be a nice way to end the week!" This is what there was: "Hey boys, here is your filter. Unfortunately, it's an unfinished state. Now put it all together so that we can tell the guys up in space how to recreate it and save their doomed lives."

The end result: they made one. Then Houston guided Astronaut Swigert through a painstaking step-by-step construction of this makeshift air filter.

The end, end result: they made it. They lived to tell the tale, then spun it off into a best-selling book and the aforementioned movie.

Doesn't seem so impossible looking back now, does it?

Now, I bring you more real-life drama. **Mine.**

The year was 1994. The month was November. And the Just For Laughs Festival was $1.5 million in debt, and without a major sponsor or an American TV deal (two factors imperative to our success). Life at the time reminded me of an old song from Chicago, one of my favorite bands, entitled "When All The Laughter Dies In Sorrow."

Things got so bad, I actually sat down late one night with Jacques Fournier, our V.P. Finance at the time, to plan the unthinkable – the Doomsday Scenario – to close down our 12-year-old event.

For this, we planned everything. What we would say to the banks. What we would say to the government. How we'd explain the closure of one of Quebec's most beloved art and cultural events to the public and the media. It was so ominous, so unthinkable, I broke into a cold sweat and hot tears simultaneously.

The next day was bright, sunny and cheerful. And so was my mood. Because on the way home the previous evening, following the Doomsday meeting with Fournier, I decided to do the impossible. I virtually transported my mind eight months into the future. I refused to be miserable.

I knew – somehow, someway – I would sign a major sponsor. I knew – somehow, someway – I would sign a U.S. TV deal. Come July, like Apollo, we would survive our 13th mission. The event would live. How, I did not know...but live it would.

So, I proceeded to live in the future. And borrowing a technique I learned from champion athletes, I visualized precisely what that future would hold (more on this important technique later). I visualized the shows we'd put on. I visualized the glowing reviews. I visualized picking up stars at the airport. And I visualized the Festival's closing press conference, where we unveil the year's results...where I visualized myself summing things up with a loud cry of "**Yahoo!**" (long before the Internet portal of the same name).

Obviously, things worked out. We signed a huge, multi-year deal with cigarette brand Craven "A" as our title sponsor (which was the subject of yet another do-the-impossible challenge a few years later when I had to face off against the government in a battle to preserve the tobacco company's sponsorship dollars). We signed our first-ever U.S. network deal with FOX. Just For Laughs 1994 set records for overall attendance and venue occupancy rates (both of which, I'm happy to announce, we bettered the following year). We closed our books with only a minor financial surplus, but it was still a surplus. We were miles ahead of a $1.5 million loss.

And, at our 1994 closing press conference, as picked up by the radio soundbites, the TV video clips and newspaper headlines, I go to scream my "**Yahoo!**"

Inspired yet? Nice fuzzy stories, perhaps, but we still have to take "the next step" in this chapter. More precisely, let's get back on the elusive path between tomorrow's outcome and today's situations.

This path is your **road-map to doing the impossible** but, its direction, its pitfalls and its roadblocks only become altogether clear once you've traveled it. And you're going to travel it twice —with your feet, eventually...but first, with your head.

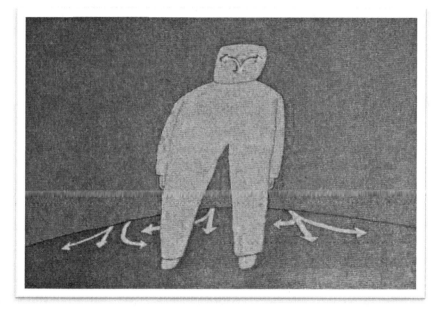

I mentioned my use of visualization earlier, which is your head's primary mode of transportation down the path. While it's lots of fun to visualize the finality, the outcome, of doing the impossible, it's not enough. You must visualize how you got there, too. And just like those pencil mazes I described earlier, you must work your way backwards.

WARNING!

DANGER!

CRITICAL POINT!

This is where many people break down in the process of doing the impossible. So before some of you jump ship and call me a charlatan, let me clear up the primary misconception about your mental march:

Of course **everything** you think about **isn't** going to ultimately happen along the path. But your thinking (here's where the "abnormal thinking" part really must kick in) will explore your many options. The deeper you go, the better chance you have of finding optimum path...or letting it find you.

This isn't quackery. An article in Wired about "How To Build a Better Body" advises:

> "Fool your neurons. The quest for perfection starts in your mind. Mentally rehearsing an action often exercises the same neural pathways as actually doing it."

Author Daniel Gilbert, Professor of Psychology at Harvard takes this even further. In his book Stumbling Upon Happiness, he explains:

> "The areas of your brain that respond emotionally to real events respond emotionally to imaginary events as well. The emotional experience that results from a flow of information that originates in the world is called feeling; the emotional experience that results from a flow of information that originates in memory is called prefeeling. And mixing them up is one of the world's most popular sports."

So...let's start playing.

Stay with me on this. Finding the backwards path is like flying a mental flight simulator. It's fun, but it's a process. Don't be lazy; visualize every possible step...and every possible subsequent outcome.

Visualize what you want to happen – the killer meeting, the convincing presentations, even the serendipity of a coincidental encounter with someone who could help. Visualize what can help make that happen – the documents, the phone calls, the midnight strolls.

Visualize what can hurt your chances – enemies, mistakes, weather, a flat tire.

While you're visualizing, note what's going on. How are the people talking to you? What are their reactions? How will they be affected by you doing the impossible?

Live the visualization with all your senses. Feel the heat. Smell the perfume. Taste the coffee. Giggle with euphoria. Shout in anger. Whisper your secrets.

Don't worry, this is not school. There is no one right answer. But before you know it, some semblance of a backwards path will form in your head.

Then it's up to you to start following it. Forwards, that is.

Note that I say "start" following it, because your backwards path isn't going to be perfect. To be frank, it'll be quite bumpy. Because on one hand, you'll make mistakes; on the other, many options you never even dreamed of will suddenly present themselves (this is what I meant when I said that sometimes, the path will find you). You must veer and persevere. Each step you take changes the optimum path...but not the ultimate result. The optimum path will only be found once you've walked it, but creating it is an on-going process.

At least you know where you're going. You're going to do the impossible. What's more, you've already been to the finish line.

Two personal examples before we close out the chapter.

In July of 1996, I was booked to be interviewed on the Cha Ba Da talk show in Montreal. Given my position at the Just For Laughs Festival at the time, these interviews were a common occurrence for me every summer, and as CEO, I was usually asked a bunch of boring questions about Festival statistics ("How many performers? How many countries? How many days? How many times can we keep asking you the same questions until you snap?"). Consequently, I usually came off as dreary and insipid; certainly not the qualities the head of a comedy festival wants to represent. If I were a viewer, I would've turned myself off in a flash.

But this time around, I decided to do the impossible — to upstage everyone on the show...including Quebec magnastar funnyman Yvon Deschamps.

And then I said to myself: Not enough! I had to go even further with my impossible and make Quebec TV history. To do this, I would have to make a scene. Well, not just any ol' scene. So I concocted this with the show's researcher:

I would come across as boring and nervous to start the interview, and I would loosen my tie as a sign of my so-called "stress." The host, the multi-talented Gregory Charles, would be perplexed. I would explain that it's a strange nervous habit of mine. Some people sweat when they're nervous. Others stutter. I, on the other hand, get undressed. And get undressed I would. All while carrying on the usual, standard, boring interview.

TV history in the making...I hoped.

Since very few guests offer to get naked on live TV (or nearly naked; I wore two pairs of underwear and dropped one), the researcher bought into the plan.

The night of the show, as I took the 45-minute highway drive to the studio, I visualized the entire interview from dreary start to impossible finish. I felt the hot studio lights. I heard the roars from the audience, and noticed some doubled over in their seats. I saw Gregory's face contorting from show and laughter. I heard the comments from the other guests, from my staff, from people on the street.

I lived the interview so many times that drive that by the time I got to the studio, it was a fait accompli. It was either going to be a television landmark, or I was going to humiliate myself, my event and my family all the way down to my as-yet-unborn grandchildren.

Well, it worked.

Phew!

It didn't just work, it worked big time. Just the way I had mentally walked it. To this day, people still come up to me on the street or in shopping malls and ask me about it. It's a great ice-breaker, a big win that still pays off.

Another big win that's still paying off is Airborne Entertainment, a mobile media company I launched with friend and Internet pioneer Garner Bornstein after I left Just For Laughs in 1999. Talk about impossible! When we started the business, family, friends—even our investors!—thought we were crazy, and that we were destined for doom. And after such great successes in both of our previous endeavors (Garner sold his previous company at the peak of the dot-com boom), the pressure to prosper was enormous.

Airborne's "Find the Path" stories are numerous, but the most gratifying was one that started at a company retreat in September of 2004. Garner and I gathered about 15 of our executive and management team for a full-day planning session, and to help motivate them, they were greeted by the following image on a giant screen as they walked in the doors of the The Willows Inn in Hudson, Quebec.

It was a fake mock-up of the front page of The Montreal Gazette, our local newspaper, and was dated Monday, September 25th, 2005...exactly one year to the day from the gathering. And the end result we were seeking, the final destination, our new impossible, was there in two-foot letters for all to see:

Montreal's Airborne Entertainment Sold in $150 Million Mega-Deal!

The Gazette

MONTREAL | MONDAY, SEPTEMBER 21, 2005 | QUEBEC'S OLDEST DAILY | SINCE 1778 | FINAL

Montreal's Airborne Entertainment sold in $150 million Mega-deal!

IN FOCUS

OLD MAN WINTER TAKES THIS YEAR OFF
On the heels of the NHL player lockout, Old Man Winter released a statement to Canadian officials declaring that he now has no reason to swing by and turn Canada into a frozen wasteland.
PAGE A16

ICE CREAM INCREASES IQ, BURNS FAT
The results of a 4 year study overwhelmingly prove that consuming massive quantities of ice cream can raise IQ levels, burn fat and ameliorate overall physical and mental health.
PAGE B12

ROADRUNNER FINALLY CAPTURED
ACME Corp. today announced that their rocket powered roller skates were used in the capture of a roadrunner that has been tearing up Arizona highways for decades.
PAGE E6

Local firm specializes in delivering fun to millions of mobile customers across North America

MONTREAL - Five years ago, their business was a blip on a virtually non-existent industry. Today, as an unequivocal leader in the burgeoning wireless entertainment sector, Airborne Entertainment co-founders Garner Bornstein and Andy Nulman are flying high as their company was sold yesterday for a whopping $150 million to an overseas media conglomerate.

The company's unique big-brand multi-product strategy solidified a powerful position in the mobile world, firmly entrenched between—and equally important to—the massive pillars of consumer/media brands and wireless carriers. In addition, Airborne's forays into direct-to-consumer distribution, both on the web and at retail, paid

Airborne Entertainment's CEO, Garner Bornstein and President, Andy Nulman, are all smiles after inking $150 million deal.

off handsomely as what was once a novelty has now gained mass-market ubiquity.

"When we first got into this field, people said I was crazy," said Nulman. "People still say I'm crazy, but at least now I have enough money to tell them

to go screw themselves". The cash and stock deal also provided Airborne's entire management team with long-term contracts and incentive clauses to ensure the company's ongoing stability and growth.

"My biggest problem," admitted Bornstein, "is

figuring out the net worth of Dennis McFern's options. This has always been one of Airborne's most perplexing conundrums. But with the advent of quantum computing, I should have an answer before the end of the decade."

Well, that was easy.

Now, all we had to do was work backwards and find our pathway to making it a reality.

Uh, the tough part.

We started by asking ourselves just what type of company would pay that kind of money for another one just finding its footing in an emerging, but unproven, industry. We figured our eventual suitor would have to be a foreign entity, one from Europe or Asia, where mobile entertainment was booming, more accepted and better understood than it was in North America.

We then asked what type of company Airborne would have **TO BE** to attract such a buyer; in essence, the corporate equivalent of prepping for "the big date." We knew we would have to solidify our finances, trumpet our major brand relationships (with household names like Maxim Magazine, the Family Guy TV show and the NHL amongst others), and lock down our crucial distribution agreements with wireless carriers.

We kept going. We postulated where we would come into contact with the foreign suitors we identified (we wanted to make it like they discovered us versus coming across as a company looking to be sold) and made plans to be *in the right place at the right time*. We role-played meetings and other scenarios of both chance and scheduled encounters. We discussed altering our product lines. We even made plans to change our business cards and website to project a new, more vibrant image.

And when we got back to the office the following day, we started walking the path forward.

The end result here? The following image, the actual front page of the Montreal Gazette's Business Section on Saturday, June 25th, 2005:

BUSINESS

THE GAZETTE | MONTREAL | SATURDAY, JUNE 25, 2005 | SECTION EDITOR: 514 987 2592

Japan's Cybird puts $110 million into Montreal's Airborne, B3

	TSX	Dow	Nasdaq	Dollar	Oil	Gold	Prime
	9866.17	10,297.84	2053.27	81.16c	$59.84	$440.30	4.25
	-2.21	-123.00	-17.39	-0.04	+$0.42	-$1.20	unch.

8 The Trading Day
9 TSX Listings
11 Mutual Funds
12 Investing Strategy

Company co-founders turned down more lucrative offers 'because we didn't want one single person here to lose their job. We want to keep our team intact'

Airborne Entertainment soars

Airborne Entertainment partners Garner Bornstein (left) and Andy Nulman keep busy in their Montreal offices. Their company is a leading provider of mobile entertainment products and applications — games on telephones.

Okay, so sue me; we were off by $40 million. But we were also ahead of schedule by three months. Sold, to Cybird, a Japanese company, no less. What still makes me shake my head in amazement to this very day is the remarkable similarity of the two images, particularly the placement of Garner and myself within them.

One an impossible dream.

The other a triumphant reality.

Amazing, if I must say so myself.

Okay, let's move on and close this chapter off with a quote from perhaps my favorite author of all time. In her epic novel *The Fountainhead*, Ayn Rand wrote reverentially:

> *Throughout the centuries, there were men who took first steps down new roads armed with nothing but their own vision.*

Of those who have done the impossible, very few have not been described as "visionary" at one time or another. Great men and women have always been expected to peer into tomorrow. The only difference with you, is that instead of just "seeing" the future, you'll actually live there...and make your way back to the present.

You've got the vision

Now, you can build your new roads.

And once you turn the page, you'll take the first step.

Leap Before You Look

Chapter 3.

Abnormal thinking.

Living in tomorrow.

Two concepts that may have sounded crazy a few days ago. But by now, you should be comfortable with the shift in logic championed by this book.

And just when you get comfortable with the absurd, I have another curve to throw at you. Ready?

You see, all the thinking in the world – no matter how abnormal – won't change anything on its own.

Before going any further, let's take a look at the cover of this book. There, emblazoned in eye-catching bold type is its title: **How To Do The Impossible**. You don't need to be Noam Chomsky (the world-renowned linguist) to understand that the most important word in the title, the operative word, is the verb **DO**.

If I had decided to call this book How To *Think* The Impossible, we'd have called it quits already and you'd be holding the back cover instead of this page.

Unfortunately, being a visionary alone isn't sufficient. To do the impossible you have to become an "actionary" as well. And that's what this chapter is all about – **action**. While everything up until this point has been designed to prepare you to do the impossible, this is where you embark on the journey of actually doing it.

And as the ancient Chinese proverb goes:

> *"A journey of 1,000 miles starts with the first step."*

So go ahead, take it. See you!

Welcome back.

In the challenging process of doing the impossible this part is – by far – the most challenging of all. By comparison, changing your way of thinking is as easy as changing your socks.

This is where brilliant ideas stall, where bold projects come to a screeching halt. This is where the future is unwritten, where the mighty are rendered impotent.

This is where doing the impossible becomes...well, impossible.

All because of the inability, the reticence, the fright, of taking that first step.

Hesitation is only natural in trying to do the impossible, because the ultimate goal is to rise above the norm, to reach previously unbeknownst heights.

And from the lofty perch of rising above the norm, the view can be terribly intimidating. Look down, and you can become apprehensive.

And with apprehension comes second thoughts. And second thoughts will pop the majestic bubble you've spent the last two chapters blowing up.

Without quick and decisive action, you'll find plenty of time to contemplate and come up with a number of arguments. All delivered by the steadfast voice or reason.

The type of arguments that any normal person would consider.

But remember, you're not normal! You don't listen to that stuff anymore!

In doing the impossible, ignorance is indeed bliss. Sometimes, the more you know, the more you don't want to know.

Still...that first step is the hardest. So what do you do?

You close your eyes. You hold your nose. And you jump.

YOU JUST JUMP.

I know it sounds elementary, but there's no other way in. You can't dip your toe into the impossible to check out its temperature.

Once again, conventional wisdom is warped. Go ahead — **leap before you look**.

Great entrepreneurs—the ballsy ones like Branson, Jobs, Schultz...even Bill Gates—have an expression for this:

READY.

FIRE!

AIM.

A sardonic take-off on the classic instructions of target shooting perhaps, but you'd be hard-pressed to find an expression more appropriate to doing the impossible.

Now this is not to say that you shouldn't have a plan. That would go against the premise of the previous chapter. But you must make the distinction between a guideline and an encyclopedia. You don't want to fall victim to the dreaded "analysis by paralysis."

I saw that disease contaminate a one-time classmate of mine, perhaps the brightest and most energetic of us all. While the rest of us university grads were busy interviewing with different corporations and invading the job market, he was busy taking courses and reading books in his endless, anal-retentive pursuit of precision-prefect resume.

Guess what? By the time he finally printed his masterpiece, the dream jobs he wanted so badly were already taken. By the rest of us. Oh well...

My first-ever marketing professor, the late Don Tobin (a sage, high-ranking corporate executive who retired and brought real-world savvy to the classrooms of Vanier College in the '70s) ingrained the pearl of wisdom into all of his students:

> *In marketing, as in life,*
> *you never have enough time*
> *or enough information.*

So when's the right time to do the impossible?

How about right now?

Why wait? Take your shot.

Now.

Or, at the risk of sounding like an old Nike commercial, **just do it** (and may you be met with the same success rate as impossiblist Phil Knight, the company's founder).

Even though this is going to come across sounding unsophisticated to the point of being ridiculous, I'll say it anyway:

DOING SOMETHING, NO MATTER WHAT, WILL ALWAYS LEAD TO MORE THAN DOING NOTHING.

Standing still limits you; jumping opens up a world of possibilities. You can always change your course in mid-flight. It's easier to re-align and to adapt once you're still moving than it is when you're standing still.

I can think of thousands of examples of doors opening, opportunities presented or insight gained because people happened to be in the right place at the right time. Unfortunately, at the time, they had no idea whether the time – or the place, obviously – was right, wrong, or whatever! (Unlike the impossible, "fate" is a past-tense perspective.)

But at least, they were there...somewhere! They took the first step; nothing would have happened had they stayed in bed. (For a personal example, I remember the night I met my wife. If was a Friday night and I was home studying. Somehow I let myself be coaxed out to a movie by a friend, who introduced me to some girl in line she happened to know, The rest is history; who knows where I'd be had I chosen to stay at home? Alright, alright...please keep all those cheap jokes to yourselves).

Still with all the above said and done, with all the advice, the cheering, the urging...it's still damn hard to take the first step. It's the most impossible step in doing the impossible.

So here's a bit more help.

First of all, a little reminder: doing the impossible is more then just a petty dream. It's not some giddy fantasy. No, nothing frivolous here. Doing the impossible is the ultimate challenge. Thus, doing the impossible should be seen as a battle.

So start drawing the battle lines.

In one corner, there's little ol' "you".

The Challenger

Heavy Underdog

Never mind being "against all odds"

They've stopped taking bets

They're too busy measuring your coffin

In the other corner, there's:

It's a fight to the finish. There are no ties. There's no mercy rule. Only one contestant will be left standing when it's all over.

And it had better be you.

From this perspective, it's easy to see that doing the impossible has become more than just a challenge...it's become your enemy!

AND WHAT AN EVIL DASTARDLY ENEMY IT IS!

Your enemy shouldn't be seen as some abstract specter; it should be cemented in your mind's eye. Your battle has become someone, something trying to do you harm, trying to impede your progress. Personify this battle! Make it an ugly, vicious, frightening enemy. Give it fangs, scars, weapons...give it anything it needs to make its threat to you and yours more substantial. Make sure you can see it clearly when you close your eyes. Make the enemy a real one.

The more real an "enemy" you battle is, the more you'll want to beat it.

Because now, there's no half way. There's no runner-up-prize.

This ain't just a business opportunity or a career decision. This is a life-and-death drama! This is about your dignity! This is about your life! This is about your future! It's kill or be killed!

Look around you. The crowds are jeering. They're taunting you. They don't believe you can do it.

Straight ahead, looking at you with disdain is your enemy.

Now...isn't it just a little easier to take that first step?

You'll note that I've been referring to "you" in the extreme singular sense.

And for good reason.

Doing the impossible is a solo match. It's not a team sport. Granted, many people will share in the final victory. The conquest will benefit many. But the reason they get to do is because of one person. The person who put everything on the line. The person who leads:

YOU!

A bit of clarification here. Yes, doing the impossible is a solo competition. You're on your own against your enemy. But that doesn't mean you're alone. Just the opposite. Other people are very important in the clash against this enemy...as long as they're used properly.

Okay, stop your hate email right now. By "used," I don't mean "take advantage of," manipulate or control. Calm down.

But let's face facts. Behind every successful solo performer – athlete, musician, business woman – is a phalanx of advisors. Tiger Woods, the world's greatest golfer, has a team of coaches. The sage Warren Buffet of Berkshire Hathaway fame makes billions for himself and money for millions, but he collects loads of information from scores of smart people before making his pivotal decisions. And where would Barbra Streisand be without people to write and arrange songs for her? One which just so happens to include the lyrics:

> *"People who need people*
> *Are the luckiest people in the*
> *world."*

Now, let me get back to where I was a couple of paragraphs ago

Despite the solitary nature of doing the impossible, the support of others is crucial. But your ultimate success depends on how you ask for, and how you use, this support. Looking for support as it pertains to "the enemy" is fine. Looking for support as it pertains to "the battle" isn't. There's a profound difference between the two.

Discussing the <u>enemy</u> is a learning process. I trust this is standard procedure in any battle you fight. Information is power. Forewarned is forearmed. The more you know about your enemy's history, its weak spots, its previous performances, the better prepared you'll be for your own personal showdown.

However, discussing the <u>battle</u> is a complaining process at best, a search for sympathy at worst. Either way, you lose.

People want you to feel needed, necessary, of consequence. By valuing their judgments (discussing the enemy) they feel important. Even if their advice isn't pertinent this time around, your qualified consideration of them will validate their time and opinion, and assure their availability next time around.

But by whining or looking for a shoulder to cry on (discussing the battle) you do one of two things:

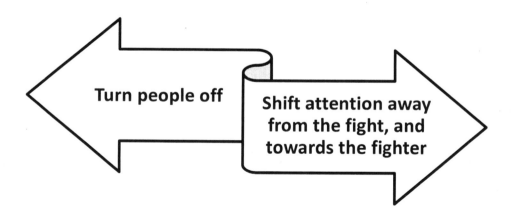

Turn people off

Shift attention away from the fight, and towards the fighter

Spouse, boss, partner, children, best friend – no matter who you discuss the battle with, no matter how close they are to you, they ain't got the solution. Some will cop the attitude of "I got my own problems buddy," and flee. While painful at first, ironically, this response is the better of the two for you. At least you're on your own again, read to concentrate on the battle.

Others will become security blankets. They'll take the battle personally and try and look after you.

DANGER!
DANGER!

They'll mask the battle in their heartfelt efforts, trying to make everything all right.

STAY AWAY!
STAY AWAY!

At the moment, it may seem like just what the doctor ordered. Their intentions will indeed be sincere.

But you need to stay sharp and focused on the battle at hand. Warm, fuzzy stuff will be your reward **after** you win.

Doing the impossible is not just a solo fight, it's an internal dilemma. You'd have to keep your emotions to yourself. Those who have already achieved this impossible have often endured periods of desperate loneliness and alienation. Sorry. But that's the emotional price frequently paid by those who see further, those who plan to do more, than others.

From here on, you are no longer "yourself"; you are an actor on Shakespeare's world stage, playing the part of someone about to do the impossible. Hey, I never said it would be easy. Nobody did.

But once you take that first step, once you take it alone, with no one there to hold your hand, you're one step close to victory.

And if just any ordinary victory is sweet...just wait until you savor the impossible.

In a book rife with radical ideas, perhaps my favorite of all is one that is almost understated when compared to its "live in the future" or "personify the battle" brethren.

Yet its ramifications can be so vivid, it alone could be the subject of a book.

Perhaps it just flew by unnoticed when I said that in doing the impossible "**you are no longer 'yourself'; you are playing the part of someone about to do the impossible.**" But this is perhaps the most savvy advice lurking between these covers.

The reason it's somewhat concealed is because, like other concealed weapons, it's powerful and dangerous. It's not for everybody. Some people are just not comfortable with taking the process of doing the impossible to such an extreme. And believe me, modifying your personality, altering your emotions, changing the way you interact with those you deal with and those you love is indeed extreme.

But to many, it works. And it works big-time.

In essence, it's the ultimate adhesion to Shakespeare's proclamation that "All the world's a stage." Yes, the world's a stage, but you're the writer, the producer, the director, the costume department, and most importantly...you're the star.

It's the ultimate creation. You create a persona, a character, who is going to do the impossible. You create his or her universe. You decide, to accomplish the impossible in this situation, what he should look like, how he should talk, what he should wear, how he should react. (I used the pronoun "he" for no other reason except that it won the pre-game coin toss. Obviously, your persona could be a "she"...whether or not you are one yourself.)

The deeper you go, the better prepared your "persona" will be for the battle.

Then, you step into the role.

Because I use the phone so constantly in my battles, what helps me maintain the many different moods of my "persona" is a mirror strategically placed beside my desk. This way, when I'm talking, I'm able to catch a quick glance and ensure that I look the way I sound. To see how effective this can be, try to do the opposite in front of a mirror right now; try and to sound angry with a big smile on your face, or vice versa. Uh-uh! If you can't convince yourself, you won't convince the party on the other end of the wire. (As an added benefit, the desk-side mirror accessory assures you'll never again be embarrassed by a bagel seed, or worse, stuck between your teeth.)

On one hand, this extreme role-playing may come across as strangely schizophrenic (what, you expected something "normal" here?). But on the other, it gives you a truly unique perspective of the impossible battle, allowing you to be deeply entrenched in it, all the while maintaining an outsider's objective overview.

It's the best of both worlds...provided you're willing to split your world in two in your quest for the impossible.

FAIL YOUR WAY TO THE TOP

Chapter 4.

There is only one more hurdle remaining in your conquest to do the impossible:

The chance that you won't.

Even after taking the all-important first step, your mind's automatic braking system sometimes kicks in at the most inopportune moment, sending you into a wildly-spinning skid. All because of one word.

The word is "failure" and the usual corresponding emotion is "fear." Unfortunately, as one comes, the other is not far behind. As a pair, they're as inseparable as politicians and scandal.

I would bet the mortgage that you've been brought up to believe that to "err" is wrong; to accept that "mistake" equals "bad"; to concede that "failure" means "stupid."

Worse yet, I'd wager double or nothing that you sometimes harbor the common, yet irrational, painful inner gnawing that your failures are somebody else's successes.

Now, the basic premise of this book should eliminate this fear completely; I mean, how can you be afraid of failing if, in your mind, you believe that you've already succeeded?

I say "should" eliminate because I can't ignore a very harsh reality. And that is no matter how abnormally-well you trained your mind, there's a glitch in your mental operating system; a glitch that can take years to reprogram. That glitch gives the option of failure disproportionate power over your other more positive thoughts. And that glitch can derail even the most swashbuckling entrepreneur.

Now, I'm not suggesting that you ignore the possibility of failure. Not at all. Knowing it exists and pretending it doesn't is a sign of psychosis, not success.

However, I do suggest you change the way in which you treat failure. Failure's merely an adult bogeyman, a gruesome creature in a dark closet ready to jump out and scare the pants off you when you least expect it.

Failure as a bogeyman. Well, doesn't it sound silly? And it **is** ridiculous! As a concept, failure has been given a lot more respect than it deserves. It's been treated with reverence, sanctity, awe...and thus, fear.

Therein, lies a key in de-mystifying and defeating failure: you must demean it. As ridiculous as this sounds, the concept of failure has become arrogant. It's starting to believe its own press releases. What it really needs is to be brought down a couple of notches.

So to hell with failure! Laugh at it.

Better yet, embrace it and welcome its possibility.

Charlie Chaplin, renowned as one of the world's greatest comedians, once said that he loaded his films with pathos to help heighten the humor. The presence of the sad scenes actually accentuated the funny parts.

And the same goes for association between success and failure. The possibility of the latter makes the former that much greater. So failure should not be feared. Instead, it should be considered a mere necessary evil in the quest for success.

But don't take my word for it. Heed the enlightened advice of this generation's most erudite philosopher – Yoda.

In The Empire Strikes Back, there's a wonderful scene where Yoda urges Luke Skywalker to remove his sunken X-Wing fighter from a swamp using only the spiritual power of "The Force." Young and impudent, Luke is obviously skeptical. After a few minutes of whining, he gets a tongue-lashing from Yoda and concedes that he'll give it a try.

That's when Yoda, in a mere 10 words, summarizes the yin-and-yang relationship between success and failure.

TRY NOT.
DO, OR DO NOT.
THERE IS NO TRY.

Either you do it, or you don't. You succeed or you fail. There's no in between. Words to live by. From a CGI character, no less.

Perhaps much of this flippancy that I personally flaunt towards failure comes from the fact that I've worked with so many stand-up comedians, and learned so much from them. For a stand-up comic, there is no such thing as success without failure. That's why at Just For Laughs, we lived by this adage:

If everything worked

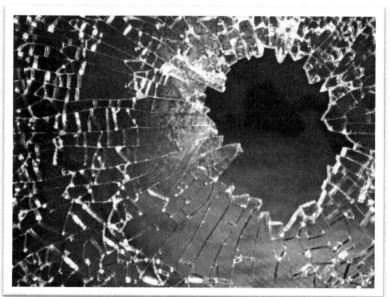

we didn't go far enough.

If we didn't have at least one flop, we knew we played it too safe, and were too conservative in our programming. As insane as this sounds, something that didn't work showed that we were doing our jobs properly. (I remember getting calls from my partner Gilbert Rozon on a regular basis asking, in the positive sense: "Did you make a mistake today?")

I also remember a particular interview on CBC's Newsworld about the art of comedy (don't worry, I kept my clothes on for this one). The show I was on allowed me to take calls from across the country, and the most intriguing question came from a 12-year-old kid from Vancouver who asked:

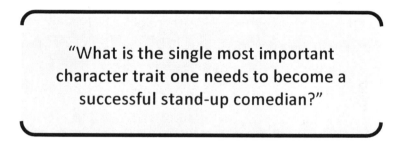

"What is the single most important character trait one needs to become a successful stand-up comedian?"

The answer was simple.

"You have to accept the fact," I told him, "that no matter how hard you try, no matter how well you prepare, the first time you get one stage you're going to stink. You will be awful. And you probably won't be much better the second time. Or the third. But eventually, things will change. Eventually, the laughs will come...but only is you get through the nights of silence. To get to heaven, you'll have to walk through hell. But if you can accept that, and if you can actually look forward to it then you chances of success increase a hundred-fold."

Only by accepting the possibility of failure and willingly embracing it can you overcome your in-bred fear of it.

And only by overcoming your in-bred fear of it will you finally be ready to do the impossible.

Let's go back to our impossiblists. Steve Jobs. Sir Richard Branson. Howard Schultz. Jim Abbott. Guy Laliberté. James Cameron. I could list hundreds more in minuscule 6-point type for hundreds of pages. But somewhere in all their stories of accomplishing what nobody before them ever has, is the same chapter – the chapter of impending doom. Don't ever, ever, forget that:

EVERYONE WHO HAS EVER DONE THE IMPOSSIBLE HAS, AT ONE TIME, BEEN ON THE BRINK OF TOTAL, OUTRIGHT DEFEAT

These aren't minor setbacks I'm talking about. This ain't a busted project here and there. I'm talking about major, ruinous catastrophes where all-impending doom is so close you could smell the rancid garlic on its breath.

My own personal success stories of Just For Laughs and Airborne Entertainment sound all hunky-dory now, but they were far from leisurely walks-in-the-park. I'll never forget the chilling times at Just For Laughs when Gilbert would gather the exec team and say: "Guys, if you own homes, better put 'em in your wives' names." Or times at Airborne when we didn't have enough money in the bank to make payroll. Or when certain investors wanted to cancel financial commitments after the tragedy of 9/11. "It's a bloodbath out there boys," one told us. "You'll have to suffer along with the rest of us."

The fact that we got through all this grief and crap made the wins so much sweeter. This is why I always proclaim that you can't win if the possibility of losing is nonexistent. Without the option of loss, life would be a continuum of wins. Sounds nice now, but after a while, win after win after win after win will become surreal. Your wins would be taken for granted and unappreciated. And life would be dreadfully boring.

Similarly, risk is a natural companion to failure. And without risk, you couldn't do the impossible. You'd do the everyday.

Success without risk is like triumph without glory. Anyone can do it.

All this reminds me of a wonderful story about risk, one which truly embodies its spirit of adventure that can't be pin-pointed down to any one source, but it's ingenious, nonetheless.

It seems that there was this philosophy professor who evaluated his students exclusively on how they did on his final exam. Your in-class participation, your papers, your attendance were worthless. Nothing else mattered except the final exam. And it was worth 100% of your final grade.

Anyway, the day of the exam arrives and there's only one question. Three words. Worth 100%. Here's the question:

WHAT IS RISK?

So dozens of students in the class start writing like mad, spewing theories from Sartre, Freud, Kierkegaard and the like onto paper in a frenzied rush.

But one girl hands in her paper after 10 seconds. She smiles to the rest of her class and walks out calmly.

Her paper reads simply:

What is risk?
THIS is risk!

There were only two choices the professor had in grading her: **0 or 100**. And as the legend goes, she got the perfect score.

I love that story. Both subtle and blunt, the parable serves to validate the concept of risk and demean the concept of failure in one fell swoop.

But these tales aren't all allegorical. I read a great story about Google in Fortune Magazine, which described the company as "a place where failure coexists with triumph." The specific anecdote was about a V.P. named Sheryl Sandberg, who made a mistake that cost several million dollars. Oooof! She swallowed hard and informed Google co-founder Larry Page of the problem. His response? "I'm so glad you made this mistake, because I want to run a company where we are moving too quickly and doing too much, not being too cautious and doing too little. If we don't have any of these mistakes we're just not taking enough risk."

(Feel free to clip the previous paragraph, put it in your wallet, and pull it out to show your own boss at the appropriate moment. Or...send your resume to Google.)

When you really think long and hard about it, failure is just another part of the process of doing the impossible...well, it is as long as you fail forward.

Failing forward is embodied by the poetic Korean adage **CHI JUL PAL GEE** which, loosely translated, means:

You fall down seven times, and on the eight you get up.

Failing forward is simply succeeding at finding a way something doesn't work. Like we saw with those pencil mazes, getting lost is not the end of the world, it's just a path which you won't be taking anymore. You can always backtrack and start all over again. This is why management guru Tom Peters says that the single stupidest statement in business is: "Why didn't you get it right the first time?" (Incidentally, "failing backwards" is making the exact same mistake twice. That's one of the few times when failure means stupidity.)

Failing forward was at the root of the Just For Laughs Festival. Gilbert launched it as an antidote to a failed music festival he had produced.

Failing forward was at the root of Airborne Entertainment as well. Garner and I first came together to start an Internet content company called Eyeball Glue. When we realized there was no sustainable business model, we switched directions over a weekend to concentrate exclusively on mobile media. Phew!

Failing forward also makes for some surprising business yarns, starring some of your favorite brand-name products. For example:

Teflon: Discovered in 1938 by accident when DuPont's Roy J. Plunkett research on refrigerants went awry. At the time, Plunkett was studying the reaction of the gas tetrefluorethylene by placing a cylinder of the gas in a cold box. When he opened the cylinder, he was disappointed to find the gas done and replaced by a waxy blob that slithered around the container without sticking to it. Sixteen years late, French engineer Marc Gregoire tried to improve the efficiency of fishing rods coating them with the substance. That didn't do much for the rods, but in the process, he discovered how to coat metal with Teflon. He coated a pan with it, opened the TFAL company in 1956...and the rest is history.

Silly Putty: Discovered by General Electric engineer James Wright during the Second World War. His was trying to find a rubber substitute to help deal with the shortage caused by the war. His invention, a mixture of boric acid with silicon oil bounced, but it also stretched and broke into pieces. It wasn't until 1949 that Silly Putty found its name and proper vocation. That's when advertising copywriter Peter Hodgson borrowed $147, bought a mammoth clump of the stuff from GE, cut it into one-ounce lumps, packaged it in plastic eggshells and sold it for $1. To the day, it remains one of North America's annual best-selling toys.

Post-it Notes – A failed 3M adhesive was adopted by the company's Spencer Silver in 1979. He applied it to little paper rectangles, enabling them to stick without really sticking. They went nowhere, except to Silver's colleague, Arthur Fry, who used the rectangles for his church choir, enabling the singers to mark their place with a paper that would not fall out, but would also not damage the fragile books. Fry also used one of the markers on a report he sent to his boss. When his boss's reply came back written on the same marker, he realized the semi-stickers could be marketed as notepads for short comments, instructions and reminders.

And so it goes. Even North America was borne of failure; don't forget that Columbus was looking for a quicker route to India when he stumbled upon our shores. No wonder George Bernard Shaw once remarked: "All great truths begin as blasphemies."

As I've said numerous times in this book, I could go on forever with examples. The point here is that failure is relative; its status changes over time. And maybe, after examining, de-mystifying and demeaning failure, we've finally uncovered its Achilles heel:

FAILURE IS A TEMPORARY STATE

Failure is fleeting. At best, today's failure may lead to tomorrow's success. At worst, today's failure is forgotten.

Let's look at a good example:

Fellow Canadian Jim Carrey

Despite the usual fable-making doctrine that labeled him an "overnight success," Jim Carrey had been kicking around showbiz for a long time before breaking into tinseltown. I first met him when I was a journalist and he was a whirlwind 18-year-old impressionist making the rounds of comedy clubs across the country. Relentlessly ambitious, he preformed everywhere he could find a stage, and everyone who came across him predicted big things for this rubber-faced lunatic.

Predictably, Jim had a brief fling in the Hollywood spotlight a few years later, starring in the vampire movie *Once Bitten* with Lauren Hutton and headlining a short-lived sitcom called *Duck Factory*. Once the movie tanked and the sitcom canceled, Jim was considered washed-up. Yesterday's news. Another failed comic. (In fact, when we tried to get Jim to co-host our Just For Laughs Showtime TV show in the early '90s, the network executives, who will mercifully remain nameless, steadfastly refused to approve him. Ouch!)

So what did Jim do, limp home to Jackson's Point, Ontario? Nope. He just started again. He took bit parts and supporting roles; a real step down from film and sitcom stardom. Then he earned a spot in an ensemble sketch comedy show called *In Living Color*. His over-the-top antics made him one of the show's highlights, and he was soon offered to star in a small, independent comedy film.

That film was *Ace Ventura, Pet Detective*. Today Jim Carrey **STILL** earns upwards of $20,000,000 per movie. Yesterday's news indeed.

Now let's look at a bad example:

Richard Milhous Nixon

Now we've all had bad days at the office, but few of 'em have been as miserable as June 17, 1972 was to ol' Tricky Dick. That's when five of his henchmen were arrested for bugging and burglarizing the Democratic National Committee headquarters at the Watergate Hotel in Washington, D.C. It was the beginning of the end. This man was the President of the most powerful nation on earth, and got caught like a common crook.

On May 9, 1974, the U.S. House Judiciary Committee did the unthinkable and opened impeachment hearings against Nixon. Exactly three months later, Nixon did the unthinkable and quit. He was the only President ever to resign while in office, and did so in a state of total humiliation, with only microbes of dignity left clinging to his fleeing butt.

Imagine the shame! He was caught lying, cheating, erasing tapes, ordering cover-ups. This was, intense, total failure; moral meltdown meets bumbling incompetence.

If failure was indeed permanent, Nixon would've been forgotten. He would've been banished to a figurative Siberia (perhaps Canada!), struck from collective memories, left to die in a phantom zone of obscurity.

Yet less than a month after his resignation, Nixon was granted an unconditional pardon by Gerald Ford. And less then a decade after the Watergate debacle Nixon resurfaced as an elder statesman! Ronald Reagan and the first George Bush turned to him for advice; he helped open up China for Jimmy Carter. He published a series of best-selling books. He was the subject of a renowned documentary series. And when he died, he was given a full state funeral service.

So much for lasting failure. I guess the old cliché is true; time indeed does heal all wounds.

Believe it or not, I remember recounting the Nixon saga in an unconventional attempt to cheer up a somewhat disheartened Sarah Ferguson, the Duchess of York, in late 1996. We were seated next to each other on a plane headed to Los Angeles, and spent a good deal of the flight discussing her situation at the time, and what the future held in store for her after a failed marriage, a number of front-page tabloid scandals (including being photographed topless), and the ensuing banishment form the Royal Family. She laughed when I said that despite all this, she was still better off than Nixon.

And she was. Even at that point, less than a year after her very public divorce, she was the author of a best-selling autobiography, part of the prestigious lecture tour that paid her more than $250,000 per night and was being courted throughout Los Angeles for different showbiz projects. And although being the spokeswoman for Weight Watchers (a deal she was then finalizing) was not the most prestigious gig on earth, it did come with a $1 million annual paycheck. Scandal? **Uh, what scandal?**

Let me repeat: time does heal all wounds. There is no such thing as lasting failure. Its status changes—it diminishes!—over time. It's a temporary state.

So, what have you got to worry about? Who's afraid of the big, bad wolf?

Come on, failure. Jump in the back seat. We're on our way to do the impossible... and you're invited to enjoy the ride.

SEE YOU AT THE TOP!

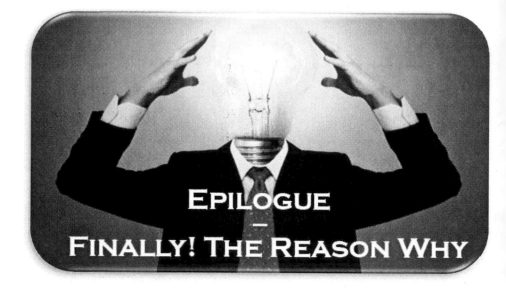

EPILOGUE
—
FINALLY! THE REASON WHY

You're almost there.

You only have a few more pages to go.

But why wait?

It's time to put this book's overall theory into practice right now. Once and for all. To prove that the minimal amount of time you invest in digesting this volume was worth its while.

So here's your challenge: go outside, grip the bumper of your car and lift it off the ground. Don't stop until you elevate it, let's say, three feet or more. If you don't have a car, lift a neighbor's or even a stranger's.

Go on now.

I'll hang around here.

Done yet?

All right, let's get to the point. Most of you didn't even attempt the lift. You presumed it was more metaphoric than literal, and you waited to see what real lesson there was to learn from such a foolish challenge. Well, there is indeed a deal lesson. (By reading this far, you kinda know what's coming, don't you?)

But before we get to it, let's get to a little story first. A little story about five skinny kids, ranging in age from eight to thirteen, in Denver, Colorado. A few years ago, just after Christmas, the five were playing in a backyard and heard cries of help coming from the street. When they went to see what the fuss was all about, they were shocked to see a Ford Escort lying on top of a trapped man.

So what did they do?

You guessed it...they lifted it off him.

The man, Gary Lewis, was changing his transmission when his car fell, crushing his chest. The kids lifted the car enough to enable him to slide free. "They definitely saved my life," said Lewis, "because I was losing breath fast."

How were these scrawny children able to perform such a heroic, superhuman feat?

"**I drink milk**," reasoned eight-year-old Shugey Shead.

"**I drink milk, too, and I eat cheese**," explained Tamika Brown, nine years old.

"**It probably had something to do with Christmas candy; all that sugar gave them energy**," rationalized Yvonne Brown, Tamika's mother.

The real reason?

They did it because they had to.

Remember the sage words of Yoda (can you believe that I'm quoting a puppet twice in one book?)

DO, OR DO NOT.
THERE IS NO TRY.

The kids were faced with two options: either a man dies, or they save him.

They did it because they had to.

Now, let's go back to our little Epilogue-opening challenge. Of course you weren't going to lift your car...even if you actually got off your butt and made some sort of attempt.

There was no motivation.

In other words, **you didn't have to.**

Now imagine for a second – and God forbid – your child was trapped under your car. Believe me, that car would fly. Somehow, from somewhere, you'd find the strength to hoist that vehicle high.

Yea, yeah, you can keep all your physicists and scientists explaining the notions of adrenaline and such. I don't want rationalizations. I want emotion.

You wouldn't lift the car because of any physiological justification.

You would do it because of emotion.

You would do it...**because you had to**.

So this brings us to the defining element of this book:

WHY DO THE IMPOSSIBLE AT ALL?

Are you doing it to get rich? To impress others? To reap revenge upon those who doubted you in high school?

Jeez, I sure hope not.

There really is only one legitimate reason to try to do the impossible.

It's because you have to.

Think back to the fallen Ford Escort in Denver and use that as a symbol of doing the impossible. Don't let it crush you. Raise it off the ground. Raise it high above your head. You'll raise more than just a metaphoric car. You'll raise your self-esteem. You'll raise a little hell. (Hey, what's the use of doing the impossible if you don't have a bit of fun along the way?)

Doing the impossible is not for others. It's not for your children, your parents or your partners. It's not for your fans, for your boss or your staff.

Doing the impossible is a gift for you.

Doing the impossible has been called "A ritual of purification; a fierce test of oneself." But, it's a test which you write, which you correct and which you, and you alone, evaluate. No peeking at your neighbor's paper.

Once you commit yourself to it, doing the impossible puts new meaning into just about everything you do.

Doing the impossible will change the way you wake up in the morning, the way you face your day, the way you go to bed at night.

Doing the impossible will change the way you act, interact and react.

Doing the impossible will change your present, but most notably, it will change your future.

Yes, doing the impossible will change the way others will look at you, but most importantly, it will change the way you see yourself.

Doing the impossible will improve upon what you see when you look in the mirror.

For no longer will you just be "you."

You'll have passed your own test.

You'll be ritually purified.

You'll have done your the impossible.

And once you actually do it, you'll bask in the warm, ecstatic aftermath that goes with it...until you tire of reliving bygone glory...and decide to do the impossible all over again.

Just because you have to.

So... what are you waiting for?

About the Author

While young in spirit and snappy in dress, Andy Nulman has been creating and leading major media projects for over thirty years.

Andy _used to be_ best known as the co-founder and CEO of the world-renowned Just For Laughs Festival; these days, as President and CMO of Airborne Entertainment, he's celebrated as a pioneer in the burgeoning mobile media space.

In his spare time, Andy is also an engaging speaker, oft-published author, inventive stage director, half-decent snowboarder, hot-and-cold hockey goalie, and prolific blogger on the art of Surprise (check him out at www.andynulman.com).

Married for over two decades to childhood flame Lynn, Nulman's greatest personal thrills come from snowboarding and playing hockey (he's a fearless goalie), but mostly from his sons Aidan Foster and Hayes Brody, and dog Shaydee. His major disappointment is that he has only one life to live...but he's working on a solution.